Create Your Own
Backyard Wildlife Habitat

Doris Dumrauf

RACCOON CREEK PRESS
Pittsburgh

ISBN: 978-0-9976767-0-9

Library of Congress Control Number: 2016910275

Produced by: Legacy Road Communications, LLC

Publishing a book is similar to planting a garden. The seeds were planted years ago, and now the efforts are finally bearing fruit. Since planting our yard with native plants, my husband and I have spent many hours observing creatures we had never seen before. I began to record the wildlife and plants with my camera. Soon I was giving presentations about the benefits of native plants.

It seemed a natural progression to publish a book. Thank you to my editor and designer, Jay Speyerer of Legacy Road Communications, for making my vision a reality.

Most of all, I want to thank my husband, Don, for maintaining the garden that gives us so much joy.

All animals depicted in this book are wild and unposed, with one exception. I photographed the permanently injured Great Horned Owl during a photo workshop at Ohio Nature Education.

This book is dedicated to all the wild things that inhabit our world.

Doris Dumrauf
May 2016

Welcome to the habitat!

Wildlife and plants need places like this to survive. Insects drink nectar from the flowering plants. Migrating birds stop over for a quick drink and a shower under the waterfall. Look closely below the water's surface, and you will see a nursery for dragonflies and frogs. Let's have a look at some visitors and see what they have to tell us.

You might hear me before you see me because my zit-zit whistle announces my arrival. In fall and winter I often travel in flocks with other cedar waxwings. Plant trees and shrubs with berries or other fruits and you might see me in your yard. I find serviceberries very tasty and can't get enough of them. Yum, yum!

Eastern Bluebird

Raising my young is hard work because they are always hungry. My mate and I spend much of our day flying low to the ground to catch crickets, grasshoppers, beetles, or worms for our hungry brood. Bird chicks need lots of insects to grow big and strong.

Hummingbird
Clearwing Moth

As a caterpillar, it seems as if I'm not doing much, just hanging around. But as an adult moth, I am unstoppable. I zip through gardens at lightning speed to drink nectar on the go. Pink and purple flowers are my favorites. I guess you could say I'm a real go-getter.

Spicebush Swallowtail Caterpillar

Those aren't eyes on my back; they're markings that help to scare away predators. I hide under a curled leaf and only come out to eat. Before long, I turn into a beautiful butterfly.

Adult Spicebush Swallowtail Butterfly

As a nymph (larva), I spend years in fresh water before emerging as an adult. My favorite habitats are shallow ponds and wetlands. I hover over the water to find my prey and can fly in six directions. Nothing escapes my big eyes, and the insects I want to eat don't have a chance.

8

Monarch caterpillar on milkweed

Whether common, swamp, or butterfly milkweed, I am the only host plant of the monarch butterfly. That means the butterflies lay their eggs only on my leaves. Their caterpillars eat my leaves, which makes them poisonous to predators. If my name weren't "weed," I would probably get more respect.

Monarch Butterfly

My fuel is nectar and I need lots of it. Born in the northern United States or Canada, I fly to the mountains of Mexico in the fall. That's pretty far for a tiny insect like me. Of course, I have to make many refueling stops along the way. Asters, golden-rod, and zinnias are my favorite fast food during my fall migration. The following spring, my grandchildren make the return trip north, touching down on milkweed to lay their eggs.

Great Spangled Fritillary Butterfly

Look closely. I'm not a monarch, although I'm often mistaken for my distant cousin. I don't make the long-distance trips they do, but I have my own unique features. My wings have kind of a checkerboard pattern on the top and silver spots on the undersides. The spots act as camouflage and help me hide, even in dappled sunlight. While most butterflies only live for about two weeks, I can live up to ten weeks, from mid-June to mid-September, delighting butterfly lovers all summer long.

White-throated sparrow in a leaf pile

I love a garden that's a little messy. During winter, I need bushes or leaf piles for shelter, and I eat the insects that overwinter in them. My favorite foods are seeds, fruits, and insects. In winter and spring, I pick seeds off the ground under plants and bird feeders.

Great Horned Owl

Hoo
Hoo
Who's there?

Don't I have big, beautiful eyes? I need big eyes so I can hunt for my prey at night. Even while I am hunting in the dark, I fly up to 40 miles per hour. I can turn my neck 270 degrees (that's a *lot!*) to find my prey: rabbits, rodents, birds, and reptiles. That makes me a very important part of a healthy habitat.

I am pretty smart because I can change my color. On a white flower I am white, and on a yellow flower I am yellow. One of my favorite plants is goldenrod. I sit around all day waiting for my prey to come to me. I don't build a web, but I trap my prey with my long front legs.

Goldenrod Crab Spider

In the backyard band, I am a background singer.

I have very long antennae so I can find my way around at night when I am most active. My favorite foods are flowers, leaves, and other parts of plants. I use my green color to hide from predators so I don't become a quick meal for bats, birds, or snakes.

American robin in bird bath

Splish! Splash! I love to take long baths because it keeps my feathers nice and clean! Without clean feathers I cannot fly very well. I need to take off quickly before a hawk or cat eats me for dinner.

Rat-a-tat-tat! I peck at dead trees and fallen logs to find my food. I am one of the largest forest birds on the continent, and when I fly, my wings span over two feet. I love to eat carpenter ants, and I get them out with my barbed tongue. It may take me days to get my reward. Here's a grub. Yum, yum!

Busy as a bee, that's my motto. I'm out and about early in the morning and stay out until late in the evening because I can regulate my body temperature. I sip nectar from flowers with my long, hairy tongue, and then I take it to my nest. Farmers like me because I help feed humans by pollinating crops. That's a pretty important job for a small insect like me. I am very gentle, but I may sting if I feel threatened, so don't come too close to me.

Bumblebee

American Hover Fly

I look like a bee, but I'm really a fly. I have two wings and hover in mid-air. That makes me look like a helicopter. I can even fly backwards. Pretty cool, isn't it? Gardeners love me because my larvae feast on aphids (plant lice) and caterpillars. As an adult, I pollinate flowers.

Eastern Gray Squirrel

My favorite foods are nuts and acorns, and I often find them at bird feeders. I will jump from a tree limb to steal tasty seeds. Then I stash them underground and eat them later. Don't even think about hanging up a squirrel-proof feeder because I have yet to meet one I can't beat.

Chip, chip! That's what I sound like. You may see me eating seeds under bird feeders, but I also enjoy eating insects, fruits, grain, and mushrooms. Before winter arrives, I carry food to my burrow in my cheeks. I am a tunnel-builder, and I carry out dirt in my cheek pouches.

Eastern Chipmunk

21

Here are some things to remember when you start your own habitat:

Water is essential for all wildlife. While birds love dripping water, they also love a nice, clean bird bath. Be sure to change the standing water often so you don't attract mosquitoes. Bird baths need to be cleaned regularly to avoid the spread of diseases.

In the western U.S., monarch butterflies overwinter in California's coastal areas. In the eastern U.S. and southern Canada, monarchs fly more than 2,000 miles in the fall to their winter habitat. Monarchs need milkweed along their migration routes on which to lay their eggs.

Dead trees and fallen logs provide food and nesting places for woodpeckers.

Insects lay their eggs on certain types of native plants, which become their host plants. Native plants (plants that grew in the region before colonists arrived) provide food, shelter, and places to raise the next generation.

Butterflies and other insects cannot survive without nectar. Be sure to provide continuous blooms from spring to fall to ensure their survival.

Let an area of the garden get a little messy. Insects and other wildlife overwinter in leaf litter or a brush pile. Birds will eat many of those insects, but the others will turn into moths or butterflies the next year.

A back yard does not have to be big to provide habitat for wildlife. To attract wildlife to your yard, all you need to offer are food, water, shelter, and a place to raise the next generation. It does not happen overnight, but soon you will discover that, in nature, everything is connected. Please check out the links on my website, dorisdumrauf.com, to learn more about creating a backyard habitat.

Have fun!

About the author

Doris Dumrauf is an award-winning nature photographer and public speaker. She has published numerous photo features in magazines and newspapers.

Doris finds many photo objects in her own yard, which is a wildlife habitat certified by the National Wildlife Federation. She lives in western Pennsylvania with her husband, two cats, and a back yard full of wonderful wildlife.

dorisdumrauf.com
dorisdumraufauthor.com